Good

Listener

Kathryn Hargett-Hsu

Some of the poems from *Good Listener* first appeared in the following print and online venues:
"Sext" — *Sixth Finch*
"Trapdoor in the Closed Circuit My Life was Meant to Be" — *Wildness*
"Vinegar" — *Sixth Finch*, reprinted in *Poetry Daily*
"We All Have Our Own", "Nearby is the Country They Call Life", "Nyhavn", "兔年", "Zuihitsu", "Symphony of a Restless Night", "North" — *ONLYPOEMS*
"Dark Peak" — *Poets.org*, reprinted in *The Southern Poetry Anthology, Volume X: Alabama*
"The Eel Question" — *The Margins*

Published in the United States of America by Frontier Poetry
www.frontierpoetry.com

ISBN 979-8-9901838-0-3

Cover design by Emelie Mano. This book cover includes design elements created with the assistance of AI tools.

Book design by Julianne Johnson.

"It's true. I'm overgrown with images. / Sometimes I hallucinate."
Good Listener stretches the imagination, each poem a fever
dream. This surrealist dive into the interior ("The interior is a
country / divided by a river & a sniper on the hill") jostles and
delights with each improbable turn. Wild but taut, electric but
cool, this chapbook disorients so it can reveal. Get lost.

—**Kemi Alabi,** Guest Judge for the 2023 *Frontier Poetry*
Breakthrough Chapbook Contest, author of *Against Heaven*
(2022)

Sonically lush, syntactically attuned and innovative in image,
Kathryn Hargett-Hsu's *Good Listener* grapples with both internal
and external exchanges. Just as one must be receptive to parrot
song, a woman "paler than summer grass, crying," and to rigs'
"drizzling music," one must also calibrate oneself to receive the
'feral silence of the past,' the "[q]uestions with no answers/ above
ground," and the 'low tune dreams hum.' Meaning, one does
not listen with one's ear alone but also with one's mind and sense
of self—even if that sense is conflicted: "I can't tell my voice
from other voices/ & other voices are always with me." Like a
soundwave, these poems vibrate, they resound, and echo back,
"silent, at times whispering/ in a tongue you hardly know." You
don't need to put your ear to these poems to hear their pulse—
they make "the position of their tongue known" into "a thousand
new words."

—**Flower Conroy**, LGBTQIA+ artist, NEA and MacDowell
Fellow, former Key West Poet Laureate, author of three books
including *Snake Breaking Medusa Disorder* (winner of the
Stevens Manuscript Prize)

Kathryn Hargett-Hsu's acutely magical verses sear through the world of poetry with razor-sharp metaphor and surprise. Funny and electric, Hargett-Hsu's poems take being alive very seriously, but renders none of us free of the great laughter that is mankind's absurdity. From "nuns who pass illicit shortbreads" to the spawning sites of eels, none of us are safe under this debut poet's gaze. Like a true bard, Hargett-Hsu's a *Good Listener*.

—**Shayla Lawson**, poet, performance artist, public intellectual, author of multiple books including *A Speed Education In Human Being*, and *I Think I'm Ready to See Frank Ocean*

Table of Contents

Sext

One day my body will eat itself
like my mother & her mother & hers.

Sunset on the prairie: a village of mildewed pods
disrobes their tufts on your fingers.

Where is the crane in your pants calling today—
is it grasping at pure idea? What trigonometry?

My mind sifts through the garden
depleted & blue, searching for the drain.

Forget-me-nots are a tired antagonism.
I am sewing instability where it is not normally seen.

Your face tightening when you enter—
tongue in the cornucopia.

The dead are bounded by rivers.
But ghosts can go where they want.

All day pawing the bruise on my collarbone...
there is something inescapably feral about me.

It wants more than this plate of salty dumplings
& a phone call to release my magpie heart.

Meanwhile the dishes plot in the sink
like prophets passing one dark eye between them.

Give it here: I will press it to the ground.

Trapdoor in the Closed Circuit My Life Was Meant To Be

I am an enthusiast of looking back. Looking
to leaving, & everything leaving represents.

In the unassuming neighborhood, nuns pass
illicit shortbreads through a slot in the monastery door,
while in the adjacent alley, I leave cuttings of myself

for another to stitch. The heat traces a coronet
of mosquitos around my head, golds my pacing eyes.

Would the parrots sing like that if they knew
they'd be shot come spring? I would, but what do I know—
I killed myself once, but it didn't take. Now I'm Lazarus in scarlet

charming the dinner guests with my talk of ghosts.
Death & I, the first fiancés, sneaking off to the bathroom

to stick tongue in ear. But desire triangulates,
thrones a tyrant of absence, it takes every tenth head.
Death's always calling a Lyft. Who will catch my shadow?

Death slit her from my ankle; now she smears
red lipstick down the throat of my past life.

Like the protagonist I weep, I make a scene,
I clear the tablecloth in one frivolous sweep.
Love, why not me? Why leave me among the bitter

fruit imported only for its scent? The old self opens
like a ribcage to the sky, & a woman crawls out

paler than summer grass, crying   *take me, take me.*

兔年

after Victoria Chang

The omen birds are sharp
in their auspicious bands.

But my eyes are still adjusting
to the new prescription:
the old one reversed.

*

Characters I confuse, quarry or ghost.
Lucky days drain their oil
on a paper towel.

*

I follow nausea's braid
downstream. My thoughts dam
the creeks of sleep.

My mother's warning: don't be the poet
chasing light down a well.

*

Sometimes I scream in my head
& a little leaks onto my shoulder.

I can't tell my voice from other voices
& other voices are always with me.

*

婆婆 could tell the future—
all it took was a hand on the stomach.

*

My selves speak different dialects
but read the same scripts.
They can never finish a sentence.

*

All my life I entered
through the back door.
How else could I have turned out?

*

No, I am not who I thought I was.
I must be the master of my mind.

*

There's no reasoning with the past,
its feral silence.

I introduced it & it doubled
so now I must kill it.

The skin makes for a warm coat.

Mei (The Intangible)

after Kazuo Fukushima

Spring comes when the robins double
& the lover prepares his plasma for harvest.

Pianissimo: there goes the hinge of a dream
running sharp through the yard, collecting dew in her palms.
By dawn she's gathered her clothes, though some days
I find a stray blouse on the grass. It's too tight
on my shoulders. On my bedroom floor,
it blooms a red horn.
                          Que sera, sera, but new day,
must you be so cruel? I'm not cut out for spring,
its promise of rebirth—the cruel lilacs reaping
from the dead another green grasp, joy erupting
with the blades of common weeds. I thread my elsewhere song
through the branches of weeping trees, tongueless
bells pointing their silence in all directions.

—Don't you ever yearn? I meant it as a joke
but an afterimage flashes around your face,
a falcon rising from the rumble strip
to sip jet trails from the sky.
                          Let us never kill again
I told the metal beast, but I have sworn before.
I let a smuggler take my breast into his mouth.
Because I photographed him as he slept, kept him
curled fist to chin, I softly murdered him;

& when he bleeds from the nose, it's my hand
that slips through the border to catch it.

Vinegar

I don't want the sting of someone with a history
like my own. I don't want the other half of my knuckle bone.
The beloved is elastic, a switch for another shore,

my face on both sides of the drachma.
If only a god's tongue has no beginning or end,
what of the bones scored for the bonfire to read?

Even when I was young, I could move things
with my mind—wanted to be impervious
to fire. Now I love the days I scorch

my wrist & breath spasms in my throat,
telling me I am here in my 24th year
& joy is blistered before it is peeled.

Joy is pickling in a clay pot in the backyard,
brine smuggled from the mainland,
delicious because it smacks of what is left behind.

I seek bloodless pleasures. This cannot be impossible;
I am not comfortable with the question.
The potted flowers droop like the eye of the first boy

who wanted me—when he took me into the closet,
I saw the veil you speak of—& just behind it,
a girl dragging her spear like a steel tail.

Then I woke with all my hands & feet.
& to God knows where, I ran.

We All Have Our Own

The past shifts behind red spray paint:
small but beautiful, if you'd like to see

I take whichever menu is offered
Be polite: buy a drink & you can watch

Voices boil, reduce

My face dips beneath an unknown meridian
& crests out of reach

                    *

Wind from the desert diverts the boats back to port
Comfort plunges to meet the water's temperature

Once the divers groped for oysters
Now only pigeons roost in the grotto

Your face, the guide says,
it's too angry for a pretty girl

Of course I smiled for him
I was a prizefighter in the last town

                    *

The church of bones is open only for worship
It's an honor to be interred in a wall.

I follow the seam of the Atlantic
through tunnels at low tide

The layman can't tell what's God & what's nature
What I can tell—

Tree: fig, almond
The princess weeping for want of snow

The graffiti says
every day someone drowns in the beautiful water

Return the way I came
An ant carrying a half-burned cigarette back to her queen

                    *

Change the ending & the position of the tongue:
now you've learned a thousand new words

My night-plotline creates heat—
I'm too tired to dance, to claim what is already mine.

The dawn streetsweepers will brush it away
Lip on throat the dinghy going down

Beautiful, isn't it?
Drown in it.

Nearby is the Country They Call Life

Interior noon. The sun like a quail egg
splatters the glass.

I dust my selves with semolina
so they don't stick,
chirping in boil-ready nests.

我 tonged onto a dish.
我, my stroke order
to memorize.

Far off the stray cats are wailing,
I'd like to join.

Always my fingers pry at openings
like hairs straggling my brow.

Shame's kill
dragged along the hardwood.

Meanwhile the empire of solitude
crests over the hill
to tax & cull.

I mean
I think I'll be alone for a while.

Nyhavn

after Pierre Reverdy

Dream of the axe & a child along the canal
The houses change color with the hour

Dawn's hands drop from its face
            Leave an opening for my own

Hunger graphites my thumb
            I smear a bit of it everywhere

My eye fermenting in profile

When I look back for you
A streetlight coughs

It is saying something about my kind

Are You One of My Kind?

Over the mountain
everyone can spell half
my name.

Blood like mine
with ammonia & salt
to bloom the coal flower.

The archer levies his payload
& separates the horizon's
red oils.

The energy to raise
my gaze by one degree:
magnolia petals
boiled into syrup.

What's left of the giants
brushed bald for view.

Chasing my tail
through the old downtown
to get my teeth
into something warm.

Questions with no answer
above ground.

I'll use every part
of what offers itself to me.

Zuihitsu

Once, you carried me
to the end of the water,
& the infinite lake
dammed into a white room.

Then I knew paradise
is a tightening circle,
a diamondback
swallowing its rattle.

*

Sometimes I hallucinate
God is a monarchic bloodstain
down the front of my shirt.

Sometimes God spits
dip into the grass,
voracious, singular,

the look in His eye saying
there is nothing private
that cannot be slit down the stomach
for the surgical theater.

*

No cell service. No cable.
We pull each other taut
over a deck of cards.

Twilight sections your face
into light & dark meat.

You call me your feast
& then I'm the carp
nailed to the deck, releasing
the cologne of flood
onto your hands.

An ace matching an ace.

                    *

If I stare long enough at one point
an abyss opens at the locus
of my looking, cinching
the color around it.

Then the face your face holds
crawls forth.

                    *

I want a new perspective.
Hold me upside-down
by the mouth.

When the alarm pulls
its forceps along our legs,
it bruises me like a child
mourning her jarred firefly.

*

Pared down to my essential part,
what could I say about beauty:
its mutability: that I am
muscle & blood all along
like any animal crossing the reservoir,

& the forest of terrorized virgins
tells nothing to the wind
pleating their leaves—

*

Sometimes I see God: some fugitive
stepping out of the water
with six eyes & the body of a crow—

It's true—I'm overgrown with images.
Sometimes I hallucinate.

The interior is a country
divided by a river & a sniper on the hill.

*

I walked down the pier
& the lake stood up
more hominid than animal.

I walked down the pier
& the center of the world
is not the navel. It cannot
be pierced with a needle
or traced with the lips.

I've seen it touching
the closed eyes of children
praying their important prayers,
though it only touched me
once, in a line of wind
that droned like a widow
pressing forehead to dirt.

I walked down the pier
& thought I could see divinity
up a column of smoke or fire,
or some human manufacture—

how do I return there—

I walked down the pier
& you will not bring it to me. I am sure.

You bring only the rigs
& that drizzling music,
pitching up
from the throat
like a hand.

Symphony of a Restless Night

after Fernando Pessoa

Time crinkled like a brown bag
given to the hyperventilating.

Yet still the night was blue,
its skeins unruptured—

no hand had come
to drag me from bed
into what prophesy I'd spun
from the window.

Like anyone, my mouth wants
to be gentle.

Still my lover told the dispatcher
She's screaming in agony.

The paramedic said I'd sleep it off,
spin together by morning.
Night's right arm itches the left.

Lonely Soares wrote,
Everything was sleeping as if the universe were a mistake.

Still I am the girl waiting
for who she should have been,
the finch smacking against the silverware

waiting for her wings
to sprout in a blitz of viscera.

Still I am the woman trembling
beneath the shock blanket
with a light shining across her eyes.

How many times has the world ended for me?

I've always been the same.
Nude in my devotion to elsewhere.
With my miraculous dreams.
My spinning sundial.

North

Hand-shaved days fall into the pot.
The water fills with starch.

I move backwards & forwards
while sleep reapplies its lipstick.

Enter: blades of twilight.

Eight inches of snow
between the angels
& my skull-cap.

I slide my knife
between the vertebrae of my belief.
Use the bones as my guide.
Borders loosened at the joint,
I can crunch light
with my fingers.

Far off I am being
stitched into the groove
of someone else's fantasy.

My dreams
hum a low tune.

*

When I was north
I ate elderberries
& read songs about the sea
as the empire of loneliness.

The laments convinced me,
their cold air & hopeless gannets.

When I was north
I dreamt of hares.
Cast stones to strike them
from my memory's dark ravine.

I'm wired to see patterns:
to turn my hip & shoulder,
to protect the neck & wrist.

& know my tells: tapping foot,
heaving chest.

When I was north
I ran through tunnels
low tide brought back
from the underworld.

A man slammed into me
like an Atlantic storm
& it made me a coastline.

Is it possible to write about north
without mentioning escape?

Or fields of lavender, forever.

               *

Death cuts its immigrant braid.

Its black hair is strewn
all through the laundry.

New year: I call off
meat again.

Balsam & cedar
ignited—green.
What lives is plastic
or feed.

I'm a bobcat squinting at fire.

There, I did it again,
lived to another winter
turning over
to show its soft belly.

Isn't it miraculous enough
to have survived here?

Still my questions follow,
a key aquiver
on the piano.

*

Dear memory—

When will you be done with me?
Every sentence
trails back to you.

I want to be pried smooth
of my callouses,
I want my feet to leave
no tracks in the sand.

Dear memory—

You've come to me
wearing that olive coat
that belonged to my mother,
brass button dislocated
in the ocean.

You startled child,
your hair is shorn
winter-dark.

& still
your lip curls—

& the caves
part their sandstone hands—

pupils dilated in low light—

Dark Peak

Peak District, 2018

November will pummel you if you let it.
      Beneath it: a stain you can't scrub off
      & gales extorting the moors. You wear
your thickest socks. On walks to the clinic,

        you stomp your reflection in crowns of rainwater.
           You arrive alone & without your shadow,
              that wet animal still pinned to a mattress in Lenton.
      When you're sober, you feel it wrest, claw-&-knee

           home to you. You don't want it anymore.
              It bleeds when swabbed. You prefer the loneliness
              that arrives in the wide expanse of days
           & piles from one appointment to the next—

      it squints at every mild face & sustains the husk
           growing around you. When asked, you answer.
           You flat mood. You deny your scent. Early on
you vowed not to spar for a stranger's last lock

of empathy, though you often mistake compassion for pity.
           On non-clinic days, you buy a ticket to Hope.
           Spray-painted sheep wander as expected.
They eat what they eat. No one expects much

        of you, dark-eyed foreigner, & how you indulge
           in their erasure of you. Wind bristles
             your cheeks' fine fur. Rain darkens the gritstone—
the moors mud. You walk slowly to avoid the cut.

But the cut isn't a cut—it's a hymenal laceration,
       & it will not abandon you just because
       you've fled to higher ground. Again,
  the slitting weight of it wrings out

  that photonegative self—not your shadow,
       but the anterior record of your shadow.
       She wears exhibits 15-19 & an olive coat.
  She trails beside you in the gusting

peat moss, at times silent, at times whispering
       in a tongue you hardly know. You would like
    to discredit this self. You would like
to indulge in the lashing & tonsure,

  to braid a jute rope & petrify her beneath brutal peat.
       Be kind to her. Like other evidence, she will
       be destroyed in seven years. She appears to you
  because something inside you wants her

    to appear—to say: yes, the ladybeetle did meander
         across the frosted window—& yes, the nurse's name
         was Natalia—& perhaps the world is kinder
    than its inscription upon your back.

  After a while, she stops whispering. Again, the glazing wind.
       Again, jute rope's open question. You continue
       to walk through misting rain—the self follows
  the rain—turn your head. Tomorrow,

she will sit beside you at the back of the waiting
       room. Together, you'll wait for a nurse
    to mispronounce your name—a woman
who believes you, & who you will never see again.

The Eel Question

Researchers have been unable to locate the spawn sites of eels but they think they're adjacent to purgatory

In Chinatown, a friend squirms at the mandala of eels awaiting its garlic skirt

When I return, the bullfrogs stare from their glass cave

I haggle for 皮蛋粥 & my Mandarin humiliates me

My mother's favorite brand of canned eel is Old Fisherman: thumb-sized filets with fermented beans to flavor her noodles

The eels of the expedition smile, cast their recursive shadows onto the leaves

Someone told me it's innately feminine to reject resolution—that the domain of woman is expansive, meditative, & resists conclusion

Here it means something about virtue to keep your moods to yourself, even if my blood demands the drama of incense & burning coals

Is infestation a supply chain issue

An East Asian nematode is threatening the European eel population

The parasite dispels its eggs through the long cavity of the eel's body, & the eel shits out the eggs, then reconsumes them through the medium of a copepod; then it collapses the swim bladder

The metaphors are so obvious they embarrass me

I wish I spoke the dialect of the re-hided drum

For a while my mother was more terrified of white strangers than the plague

What do you even say to that

When I left Chinatown, a man leaned out of his car window & barked at me—the second time in twelve hours

You could gaze into the pool of shame & plunge your arm into it, & if you reach far enough you'll spawn into the guts of wet soil, somewhere close to revelation or sex

Like how the most intimate way to know someone is to hold their organs in your hands

In Trieste, Freud slashed hundreds of eels in search of testicles

Covered in red & white blood, he wrote to a friend: *All I see when I close my eyes is the shimmering dead tissue, which haunts my dreams*

Glass—gossamer—one long thrumming muscle & a disintegrated stomach

How are you going to honor the bodies that live in your body? someone asks—& all I can think is what I want for my next life: squash flowers, fish that feeds other fish

The ouroboros says *the problem with everything is death*

When eels return to the open ocean, they're electrified for thousands of miles by fat reserves alone

Can you blame the dead for believing they were rays of sun

Good Listener

I slept on three-quarters of a bed. I woke with the moon
& entered my dreams into evidence: dissolvable, tasteless sheets.
Everything smelled like pepper—like insulting flowers—
& the problem with sweetness. I was good at laundering my face.
I was just beginning to understand how to look at someone
without perceiving or recognizing them—alone, until I wasn't,
spurned from dinner dates where the men ordered more bread
& told the waiter *She's with me.* It wasn't love,
but it was dry & expanded in the cold. Rarely did we speak
of that rumor about lust, that it leaks from the same domain as blood.
When the men came to my room, we broke into our bodies
like punch-drunk looters. Harry was the longest—older—
we didn't care about each other.
When I was with him, I wanted to be ordinarily miraculous,
sewed into a periwinkle dress & set too close to the fire.
When he called me his sweetheart, I gnawed the grit & bone.
I rarely think of Harry outside of a sequence: slow noose,
seltzer splashed onto trainers, crackle of chest hair against my lips.
My mouth, disordered by rain, falls across the disarray of years
& returns textured, nipped at. Who can say why some ghosts are kept to row
in our rivers of neurons, bristling when brushed by some familiar chord—
or why some go straight to the bloodstream. Has anyone ever slapped you
because they were enraptured with your skin? I never learn.
The English say I speak English good, so I flash my glamorous teeth.
Me with my little list of commands. Me bending with my excavating hook.
Like all light-driven things, I bloom on cue. Oh, chickadee.
I've spent too long apologizing to the dead; like grief was ever a part of it.

Acknowledgements

Some of the poems from *Good Listener* first appeared in the following print and online venues:

"Sext" — *Sixth Finch*

"Trapdoor in the Closed Circuit My Life was Meant to Be" — *Wildness*

"Vinegar" — *Sixth Finch*, reprinted in *Poetry Daily*

"We All Have Our Own", "Nearby is the Country They Call Life", "Nyhavn", "兔年", "Zuihitsu", "Symphony of a Restless Night", "North" — *ONLYPOEMS*

"Dark Peak" — *Poets.org*, reprinted in *The Southern Poetry Anthology, Volume X: Alabama*

"The Eel Question" — *The Margins*

I am deeply grateful to everyone that has given my work a warm home. <3

KATHRYN HARGETT-HSU received her MFA in Writing from Washington University in St. Louis. Born and raised in Alabama, she is the recipient of fellowships from Kundiman, Disquiet International, Fine Arts Work Center, Virginia Center for the Creative Arts, Bucknell Seminar for Undergraduate Poets, and Mendocino Coast Writers Conference. Most recently, she received the Academy of American Poets Prize and the Lynda Hull Memorial Prize. Find her in *Poetry Daily, Best New Poets, Pleiades, The Hopkins Review, MQR Mixtape, swamp pink, Sixth Finch, Diode Poetry Journal, Arts & Letters, Muzzle Magazine, The Margins, Hayden's Ferry Review, The Adroit Journal*, and elsewhere.

www.ingramcontent.com/pod-product-compliance
Lightning Source LLC
Chambersburg PA
CBHW070453130626
46553CB00006B/2399